CW01367741

Therapeutic Parenting in a Nutshell
Positives & Pitfalls

A concise overview for anyone caring for a child who has suffered early life trauma, and their supporting professionals.

By Sarah Naish

THIS BOOK CONTRIBUTES TO PART OF THE
DIPLOMA IN THERAPEUTIC PARENTING

A UK LEVEL 3 NATIONAL QUALIFICATION

Inspire Training Group

First published 2016 by Amazon
Produced in association with Inspire Training Group,
Part of Fostering Attachments Ltd

www.inspiretraininggroup.com
Training, Inspiring, Healing

Copyright © Sarah Naish 2016

ISBN: 13-978-1533592156

All rights reserved. No part of this publication may be reproduced, copied, stored in a retrieval system or transmitted in any form or by any means electronic, mechanical, photocopying, recording or otherwise without prior written permission of the copyright owner.

About the Author

Sarah Naish is a therapeutic parent of five adopted siblings, former foster carer and social worker.

Sarah used her own experiences to set up and run her own therapeutic independent fostering agency, which also included specialist residential units for children with severe attachment problems. The agency was awarded an 'Outstanding' grading by Ofsted (2013-2104) in recognition of the successful therapeutic model (the T.R.U.E model) devised and implemented by Sarah. As a result she won 'Woman of the Year' in the Women in Business Awards 2014.

Sarah is now a trainer and author, running Inspire Training Group, (part of Fostering Attachments Ltd). The company is funding research into compassion fatigue (blocked care) in foster care with Bristol University. (The Hadley Centre), due to be published in autumn 2016.

Sarah also speaks at conferences and seminars helping parents, carers, social workers teachers and other professionals to heal traumatised children, overcome blocked care and to work more effectively together.

Also by the Author

Guide to Therapeutic Parenting (Community Care Inform service)

William Wobbly and the Very Bad Day

Sophie Spikey has a Very Big Problem

Rosie Rudey and the Very Annoying Parent

Charley Chatty and the Wiggly Worry Worm.

(These therapeutic parenting children's stories were co-authored with her eldest adopted daughter, Rosie Jefferies. Publication October 2016 by Jessica Kingsley Publishers).

Contents

Chapter		Page
	Introduction	6
1	What do we actually mean by 'Therapeutic' Parenting?	7
2	Why do some children <u>need</u> Therapeutic Parenting?	10
3	The Therapeutic Parenting 'difference'	13
4	The additional challenges faced by Therapeutic Parents	23
5	The impact of blocked care (compassion fatigue), and blame	30
6	The T.R.U.E model of Therapeutic Parenting- Implementing meaningful support	39
	Conclusion	43
App A	Therapeutic Parenting differences- Quick reference chart	45
App B	Author's own resources- video and web links.	50
App C	References and bibliography	51

Find us on Facebook

Therapeutic Parents

Introduction

We are all working together to try to heal children aren't we? Well sometimes it does not feel that way.

In our training throughout the UK, carers tell us that they feel blamed, judged, misunderstood and isolated. Many carers feel that supporting professionals, such as teachers, social workers and therapists, do not understand the scale of the task with which they are faced.

Similarly, when we speak to social workers and their managers, they also express a sense of frustration that their strategies and advice are often ignored. They tell us that they often feel that they are not 'on the same page' as the foster carer/adopter and other carers, looking after children who have suffered early life trauma.

Social Workers sometimes tell us how difficult it is for them to ensure that the child's best interests are kept at heart, whilst also trying to balance heavy workloads, and attend training, in order to understand developmental trauma and therapeutic parenting.

Many carers and supporting professionals tell us that they struggle to find the time to read books which will help them to underpin therapeutic parenting. For this reason, I have written this brief overview, which contains all essential information with links to further learning. Most of our resources are video based and cut down into bite sized pieces to fit into our busy lives.

This concise handbook, will explain to all parties, the underlying structure of therapeutic parenting, how we implement it, why we use it and what it does. We also explain the very real psychological problems encountered by carers, and the best way for supporting professionals to help them. By helping therapeutic parents and their supporters to gain a better understanding **of** therapeutic parenting, we can work more quickly and effectively towards improved outcomes for all our children.

Chapter 1:

What do we actually mean by 'Therapeutic Parenting'?

Therapeutic parenting is a term commonly used for foster carers, adopters and kinship carers who are looking after children who have suffered trauma, normally through early life neglect and/or abuse.

> **"Therapeutic Parenting is a deeply nurturing parenting style, with a strong foundation in empathic responding"**

Therapeutic parenting, (sometimes called Therapeutic Re Parenting), is a different way of life. Carers need to LIVE as therapeutic parents with their children. It is not something carers can choose to dip in and out of. The therapeutic parent will live a life which is well structured with strict routines and boundaries. There are no surprises, spontaneous outings or room for doubt. Therapeutic parenting is also effective for securely attached children, so there does not need to be any conflict in parenting style, if a carer also has other children.

The aim of therapeutic parenting is to enable the child to recover from the trauma that they have experienced. This is done by developing new pathways in the child's brain to help them to link cause and effect, reduce their levels of fear and shame, and to help them to start to make sense of their world. The short video 'What is Therapeutic Parenting' gives a concise overview. *(video (b) Appendix B).*

> **"An empathic, therapeutic response is the cornerstone of Therapeutic Parenting"**

One of the most popular model of therapeutic parenting currently being used in the U.K. is 'P.A.C.E'. This model was developed by Dan Hughes PhD.

P.A.C.E stands for;

- Playfulness
- Acceptance
- Curiosity and
- Empathy

In his book *(Building the Bonds of Attachment - Awakening Love in Deeply Troubled children, ref i)* Dan Hughes, talks about 'The Attitude' that therapeutic parents need to have to help a hurt child. The idea of 'The Attitude' is to facilitate the capacity for love and fun.

Other therapeutic parenting models in use are;

TBRI, (Trust Based Relational Intervention- Dr Karyn Purvis)

Safe Base Parenting Programme

T.R.U.E (Therapeutic Re Parenting Underpinned by Experience/ Empathy)

All models have the foundation in empathy and acceptance in common.

When Therapeutic Parents work in this way, they can achieve excellent outcomes, even in the absence of any other parenting strategies. It may be challenging to accept a new parenting style idea, but it can make a huge difference to the parent/child relationship, and also for the outcomes for the child. In order for therapeutic parenting to succeed, the following foundations are necessary;

Carers and supporting professionals must understand the effects of early life trauma on the child, including brain functioning, developmental trauma and attachment difficulties

- The child's __actions__ need to be interpreted correctly and understood by the carer and supporting professionals
- The child's history, as far as it is known, must be available to the carer

- The carer needs to have the capacity to react consciously and with empathy, to the child's behaviour, rather than emotionally.
- Supporting professionals must understand what the carers are trying to achieve, and demonstrate empathy for that task.
- The team around the child need to demonstrate an openness to therapeutic parenting techniques, and support each other with consistent boundaries and excellent communication.
- The carer and supporting professionals, must understand, be able to recognise and manage compassion fatigue/ blocked care in the carer.

Therapeutic parents do not need to have degrees in psychology, nor do they need to have practised as child psychotherapists! They do not even need to have previous parenting experience. Prospective therapeutic parents may be identified by;

- High levels of resilience
- Attachment style interview (ASI) during assessment
- Their interest in attending training/ discussions about therapeutic techniques
- Having enthusiasm for own learning about P.A.C.E and other relevant therapeutic models
- Demonstrating an ability to access empathy when under pressure
- Being predisposed to having natural curiosity rather than assuming behaviours are personal, i.e. designed to annoy or hurt the carer.
- Demonstrating a genuine desire to fully understand their child's behaviour and where it stems from.

Chapter 2

Why do some children <u>need</u> Therapeutic Parenting?

Many of the children we look after have not had their needs met in early life, either through trauma, abuse and/or neglect. Practitioners will be familiar with this and are aware that many of the children we care for have attachment difficulties. These difficulties mean that the child cannot interpret the world in the same way as securely attached children can. Attachment theory is a good place to start exploring this. *(Dept. of Education - Early Childhood Trauma link at ref xiv)*

The short video, (a) 'Understanding Your Traumatised Child, *(link in Appendix B)*, gives a good explanation of how early life trauma affects the child's development and later life functioning, as does 'The Body Keeps the Score' Bessel Van Der Kolk (ref vi)

One of the overriding physiological responses to trauma and stress is the increased levels of the 'stress hormone' cortisol, often referred to as the 'fight or flight' hormone. Traumatised children have high levels of cortisol which *'can have a negative impact on the physiology of the brain'* (Woolgar, 2013; ref ix)

Children with high levels of cortisol will demonstrate anxiety and fearfulness. Typically they may be considered to over react, be aggressive, over controlling, hypersensitive etc. Traumatised children are very adept at reading facial signals of others and quickly adapting their behaviour to ensure their own survival. The behaviours may continue long after the threat has passed.

(Fig 1) The fake smile - An example of one of the embedded 'survival strategies' is the 'fake smile'. (left). This grimace was used by the child in a fear state in an attempt to keep themselves safe. Long

after they are placed with new carers, the fake smile will still be seen multiple times, on a daily basis.

Dr Bruce Perry *(ref x)* states, *'During the traumatic experience, these children's brains are in a state of fear-related activation. This activation of key neural systems in the brain leads to adaptive changes in emotional, behavioural and cognitive functioning to promote survival'.*

Unfortunately, once the threat has passed and child is in a safe environment, they cannot 'unlearn' the hardwired physiological responses active in their brains. It is useful to imagine the child's base brain (amygdala) as a faulty smoke detector. Always going off at inopportune moments, even when there is no smoke, let alone a fire! Therapeutic parenting, effectively 'switches off' the smoke detector and rewires it, so that it only goes off when there is an actual threat.

The picture below from the Bruce Perry website *(ref x)* shows the brain scan of a six year old child, three years AFTER he was removed from an abusive/ neglectful situation. The dark areas are where normal brain function is absent. Synapses have failed to connect and whole areas of the brain, including language, linking cause and effect, memory etc. are affected for the LONG term.

Photo: Source: Dr Bruce Perry

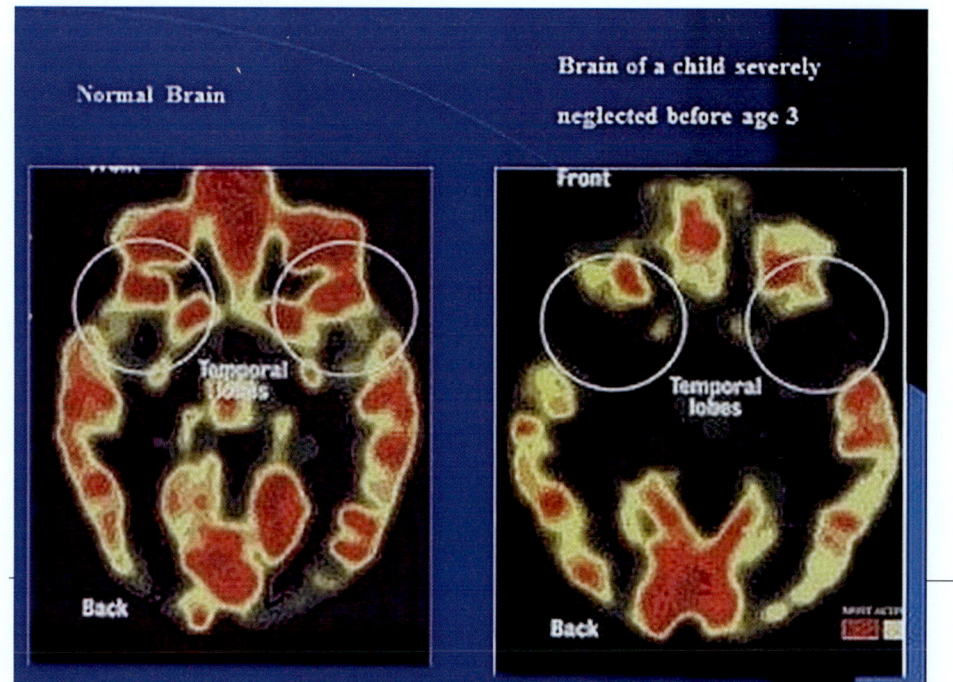

(Fig 2) MRI Scan

There is more information about the impact of neglect on brain development in 'Early brain development and maltreatment- Dept. for Education 2014 UK. *(link at ref xii)*

Therefore- Children who have suffered trauma and neglect, need a different kind of parenting to help them to 'rewire' the 'smoke detectors', and to build new pathways in their brains.

Chapter 3

The Therapeutic Parenting 'difference'

Therapeutic Parenting mainly differs from other parenting styles because it has an *enhanced level of therapeutic responses and empathy* within the parenting style.

For those of you pressed for time, I have included a 'quick reference' table at Appendix A.

Looking from the outside in, Therapeutic Parenting may appear harsh. The reason for this, is that it needs to be more structured than standard parenting. The Therapeutic Parent will also allow the child to experience 'natural consequences' in order to help them to link cause and effect.

In 2009 Adoption UK published an evaluation of training methods, *(Training Evaluation with the Hadley Centre ref xi)* it stated *'adoptive parents often use disciplinarian techniques currently popular with the media – with potentially disastrous results'*. This research demonstrated that children who have suffered trauma may be re traumatised by parents using standard, disciplinarian approaches to parenting.

We are all familiar with standard 'good parenting' techniques, advocated by social work and health professionals, so here I will explain the similarities and differences between 'standard' parenting and 'therapeutic' parenting.

Similar but *enhanced* aspects

Use of empathy- Standard parenting will use empathy to support children, however the therapeutic parent will use empathy to underpin **most** interactions with the child, and also use it as a precursor to disciplinary measures where possible. The therapeutic parent uses empathy to;

- Firstly establish a connection to the child and

- Secondly reflect back to them what they are experiencing;

IE 'I can see you are finding this difficult'.

Dan Hughes states, *'The parent should empathise with the child before putting any disciplinary measures in place and throughout the employment of those measures (eg, consequences). The parent must be genuinely empathic, not flippant.'*

The Empathic Response video (d) *(link in Appendix B)* shows a role play of a therapeutic parent, giving an empathic response to stealing. Dr Amber Elliot's book Why Can't My Child Behave? *(Ref vii)* is a good source of empathic strategies.

Routine – The Therapeutic Parent will implement a strong routine from the outset. This strong routine is largely inflexible, as the purpose is to allow the child to feel safe and to be able to predict their life, maybe for the first time. Meal times are normally very fixed with everybody sitting at the same place at the table. Children would also have their own cutlery and crockery assigned to them. They are able to identify their place in the world, have visual prompts to reassure them that they will have food, and their fear of 'invisibility' lessens. Similarly when travelling in vehicles, children should be assigned their own 'permanent' places in the car, with their own seat, and perhaps a favourite blanket or cushion left in their place.

Having a strong routine lessens the children's stress response, keeps their 'fight flight' (smoke detector) response under control, and ensures a safe predictable environment. Difficulties are often encountered at school when there is a change of routine, I.E. at the end of a school term.

Boundaries - The boundaries which Therapeutic Parents put in place will also be very firm. The Therapeutic Parent cannot allow a child to do something today, which he was not allowed to do yesterday, or vice versa. Any changes to boundaries needs to be done slowly and carefully as the child develops.

Playful response – Most parents will be playful with their children at appropriate times. The Therapeutic Parent, purposefully uses a playful response where they notice a child is dysregulated. The child's brain cannot experience fear and joy simultaneously, so by instigating a joyful response, the fear underpinning the dysregulation is diminished. Playfulness in this context, is NOT about 'playing' with the child. It is a spontaneous, unexpected 'silly' intervention. An example of therapeutic 'playfulness' is given in the video (b) 'What is Therapeutic Parenting'? *(Link in Appendix B).*

Conscious response – All parents know that it is desirable to respond to children in a measured and thoughtful manner, without acting on sometimes overwhelming feelings of anger. The Therapeutic Parent practices this many times a day until it becomes a way of life. To observers, this may appear cold or calculating. Please see *video (c) in Appendix B Contrasting Emotional and conscious/empathic response*

Acceptance – Therapeutic parents are faced with a myriad of challenges with the behaviours traumatised children present. In standard parenting we often talk about 'separating the child from the behaviour',

IE *'That was a naughty thing to do.'*

The Therapeutic Parent has to go much further with this. The behaviours are more entrenched, more frequent and often very difficult to understand. Using phrases such as 'I know you have a good heart, so I was really surprised that you......' are effective.

'Standard' parenting methods avoided by Therapeutic Parents

Asking why- Therapeutic Parents avoid asking the child why they behaved in a certain way. The child is unable to provide the answers and may feel more fearful if they are asked to provide explanations to the parent, as well as feeling anxious about the fact that the parent does not understand their behaviour either.

Lengthy conversations about behaviour- In general the Therapeutic Parent would not be sitting down for long periods of time to talk to the child in depth about their behaviour, as the child is likely to say 'what the carer wants to hear', without facilitating any fundamental change to the behaviour. We know that children who have been traumatised are very adept at saying the right things, in order to make the parent stop questioning them.

Over praising- The Therapeutic Parent avoids 'over praising' their traumatised child, in order to reduce the risk of provoking strong conflicts to the child's internal view of themselves, (internal working model). This may lead the child to feeling that the carer is lying or unsafe. For example, if the child produced a drawing, the Therapeutic Parent would not say it was 'wonderful' and place it in a position of pride. This may well lead to the child destroying the picture. The Therapeutic Parent gives a muted interested response, such as, *'That's an interesting picture, what is that bit there'?* The same applies to complimenting the child on their looks or other positive features. This needs to be done in an understated, evidence based way. For example, *'I know you have a good heart as I saw you helping Alfie earlier on'.*

Avoiding Surprises – As surprises mean that something out of the ordinary is happening, this would lead to a change in routine. The child's 'smoke detector' is over active and a 'surprise' would normally lead to higher levels of fear and dysregulation. If the Therapeutic Parent has planned a nice event for the child, they would normally inform the child very close to the event happening, ie a matter of hours or preferably, minutes.

Spontaneity- In a similar way the Therapeutic Parent is unlikely to be able to act spontaneously as routine and predictability are key to the child's feelings of security. This means life can be very dull and boring for the parent! Holidays, in particular are a challenge. Therapeutic Parents often choose to take holidays in the same place, even in the exact same accommodation, to avoid the child becoming too dysregulated and unable to manage their anxieties.

Time out/ sending to room/ naughty step – are not used in therapeutic parenting as exclusion may replicate early abusive situations, and places a reliance on the child being able to self-regulate. This is unrealistic. Furthermore, the distress caused to an already traumatised child is a disproportionate punishment.

Unrelated consequences – i.e. writing lines, having a favourite item removed for rudeness. These consequences do not help the child to link cause and effect, and are likely to increase conflict between the carer and child. This can be particularly problematic at school, if consequences are not related to actions. IE a detention for talking in class. This makes no sense to the child and does not help healing.

Saying sorry- the Therapeutic Parent does not expect or insist on any kind of meaningful apology from a traumatised child. Instead the child would 'show sorry'. This is explained in the next section.

Reward charts- Generally Therapeutic Parents would avoid reward and star charts, as this can cause conflict with the child's internal working model. IE, the child may feel they are 'bad' or worthless'. When a reward is given and the implication is that the child is 'good', the child's instinct is to realign those around him with the view they are more familiar with. 'I need to remind you I am bad'. This is an unconscious action.

Children who have suffered developmental trauma have a strong instinct for survival. They quickly learn to exploit reward charts, making them redundant, and leaving parents and carers frustrated.

Removing important rewards – Therapeutic Parents avoid punishing a child by removing an important reward or treat. This is because it is recognised that the child may well feel 'unworthy' of the treat and attempt to sabotage it, thereby reminding the carer of their 'badness'. The Therapeutic Parent would still give consequences for the negative behaviours, but would make the child aware that they thought them 'worthy' of such a reward, even though the child was 'doing their best' to have it taken away. NB: The Therapeutic Parent may then be criticised for being 'too soft', and this may be confused with an idea that the parent is not keeping good boundaries. This is unlikely to be the case.

Additional techniques specific to Therapeutic Parenting

Making it right/ showing sorry- The Therapeutic Parent gives the child opportunities to 'make things right' and 'show sorry'. For example if objects were thrown, the child would be expected (and 'helped') to pick them up. If the child hurt someone, they might be guided to rub in 'special healing cream'. Kim Golding *(Nurturing Attachments Supporting Children who are Fostered or Adopted ref. ii)* has written extensively on this.

Emotional age response- Generally responses are made which are appropriate to the child's <u>emotional developmental age</u>, rather than their actual age. It is unhelpful to think about a traumatised child's chronological age, and what they 'should' be doing. This places undue pressure, and unrealistic expectations on the child, carer and school. We would not allow a 3 year old to have unlimited internet access for example, so a Therapeutic Parent would strongly resist a 16 year old, functioning emotionally at 3, the same privilege.

Natural consequences- The therapeutic parent allows 'natural consequences' to occur to help the child to link cause and effect. For example the child may choose to spend all their pocket money instantly. The carer would not intervene and lend additional money if a sudden urgent 'need' for more money was discovered! A note of caution here. Safeguarding concerns will (and should) arise where the carer has become fixated on 'natural consequences' and begins applying them too harshly or rigidly with no nurture or empathy attached. For example;

Child wets bed. Carer makes child wash sheets in bath by hand, and says this is 'natural consequences'.

This is **not** the correct use of 'natural consequences'. This action would humiliate the child, and would be unlikely to have any effect on an event which is almost certainly beyond the child's control. Any strategy used to deliberately invoke shame is not a therapeutic parenting strategy, and would rightly be considered abusive by supporting professionals, (and indeed Therapeutic Parents).

Predictability – As routine is key, and surprises/ spontaneity are avoided, this often has implications for events such as treats and outings. A good therapeutic parenting technique is to tell a child of a change or outing very close to the time of departure, this leaves less time for anxiety and stress. This strategy is often at odds with some carers and supporters who feel they should give the child 'as much notice as possible' to prepare. We always advise parents to think carefully before issuing a threat or a promise, as they will need to see it through!

Therapeutic Parents MUST say what they MEAN and mean what they SAY!

Additional nurture- Opportunities to create additional nurture are prevalent in the home. For example a bottle or comforter may be offered to an older child. Furry blankets and soothing music may be used frequently. In our own home we had unbreakable ornaments with a mother/child/ nurture theme, furry throws and cushions and usually had classical music playing quietly in the background.

'Being the Steam Train'- Nancy Thomas *(Love is not enough)* talks about being 'the queen of the house'. The Therapeutic Parent has to be seen to be safe, secure and 'in charge' at all times. Think serenity! Expressed doubt will lead to feelings of insecurity in the child and a very fast decline into chaos and fear. I often considered myself to be the steam train, running along the track, pulling my five little carriages. The carriages would do their best to 'de rail' me, or jump on to an adjacent track and start going off at a tangent. Part of the conscious therapeutic response, is about staying on track, and keeping on moving forwards. (*Video (b) 'What is Therapeutic Parenting' in Annex B*)

Time in- The child is asked to 'stay close' to the carer, so they can be 'kept safe' at times of dysregulation. This may be difficult for parents to do when they are feeling upset by the child's behaviours. Therapeutic Parents become Oscar winning actors! Time in, helps the child to feel calmer and replicates some of the early lost nurture. Times when we would normally have kept babies and toddler close by, to keep an eye on them.

Curiosity/ 'Naming the need' – The carer will always be aware of the child's early life experiences and help them to make sense of the resulting behaviours. The therapeutic parenting children's books series *(William Wobbly and the Very Bad Day etc. Naish and Jefferies Appendix C ref xvi)*, name the need within the stories by relating the child's current behaviours, back to their past and providing the child with an explanation about where the behaviours might come from. Sometimes carers worry that they might 'guess wrong', however during training we explain that it is better to make a 'best guess' than to ask the child why they did something. Children will invariably say that the carer is wrong and deny emphatically any link, but by watching their behavioural changes over a few days, the carer can gauge how close the explanation might have been. An example of this strategy is given in the *video (e) 'Naming the Need' and also within 'What is Therapeutic Parenting'? (Links in Appendix B)*.

Nonsense questions –limited response- The Therapeutic Parent will make a distinction between 'nonsense chatter/ questions and genuine expressed thoughts and feelings. The carer will also help the child to regulate themselves and reduce 'nonsense chatter', by perhaps asking them to write the questions down, or devoting a small part of the day to listening to the 'nonsense chatter'. This may appear harsh to outsiders, but actually the carer is helping to 'retrain' the child's brain, as the child is often unaware of the extent of the 'nonsense chatter' and is usually unable to hear or absorb answers. This is easily seen when the child is asked to write the questions down. The child is usually unable to do so as they have to then use their 'higher brain' to think about the questions in order to write them down.

A short video (g) tutorial on this subject is available from Inspire Training Group. *(Link in Appendix B)*.

The following case study compares and contrasts standard parenting response with a therapeutic parenting response.

Case Study 'Callum': Application of differing parenting responses

Standard parenting response

Callum, age 8, comes home from school with holes in the cuffs of his jumper where he has chewed them.

Carer feels frustration. This is the second time this week, and it is a new school jumper. What will people think of her? In the early years, as an inexperienced carer using standard parenting techniques, Callum appearing with holes in his new jumper might have elicited a standard response from the carer such as –

'Why have you made all those holes in your jumper? I only bought it last week'!

Callum looks at his jumper and see the holes, seemingly for the first time, flies into a rage and is overwhelmed by shame. An incident follows.

Therapeutic Parenting Response

Callum comes home from school with holes in the cuffs of his jumper where he has chewed them.

USING CURIOSITY- The carer thinks – 'In his early life perhaps he used to over suck his thumb, clothing or pyjamas in order to try to get some nurture or comfort'.

USING CONSCIOUS RESPONDING- The carer may still feel a high level of frustration about the behaviour, but they respond consciously, not emotionally to the child.

USING EMPATHY - The signs of distress are the holes in his jumper. When we think about early lost nurture and the way that babies put everything into their mouth, it's quite an easy leap to see why a lot of the damage is caused by chewing and biting.

As carers became more skilled in therapeutic parenting, they are more able to give an empathic response;

"Oh dear Callum. It looks like you have had a few worries today. There are a lot on new worry holes in your jumper". (Said with empathy, not sarcasm)

NAMING THE NEED. If appropriate, the Therapeutic Parent might add, "When you were very little, you didn't have very much to do in your cot and I think you chewed things, so now you do this when you are worried, scared, or just day dreaming".

The parent then gives the child a handkerchief with her scent on for him to chew if he becomes distressed. The Therapeutic Parent will not be surprised if the child comes home tomorrow with more holes, and forgets to use the handkerchief as she knows it will take a great deal of repetition to change this behaviour.

When the child smells the scent, it is likely to reduce feelings of fear and 'calm his lower brain', thereby reducing the chewing behaviour.

Dan Seigal's book, 'The Whole Brain Child, *(ref Viii)* gives an excellent overview of the neurobiology of attachment and also gives detailed examples of empathic therapeutic parenting strategies within the book and work book.

For carers and supporting professionals, wishing to understand more about Therapeutic Parenting and applying P.A.C.E we provide a certificated online video based course (f), 'Therapeutic Parenting P.A.C.E in Real Life'. *(Link in Appendix B).*

Chapter 4

The additional challenges faced by Therapeutic Parents

Throughout our work as trainers in the UK and within our research into the experiences of foster carers, *(ref xiii)* we have found common themes about the challenges carers and parents face when attempting to implement therapeutic parenting strategies.

Naturally, the overriding desire of carers, social workers, teachers and other supporting professionals in the field, is to avoid placement breakdown and improve outcomes for children in the care system. Below I have outlined some of the common conflicts, misunderstandings, miscommunications and other numerous challenges, experienced by all parties when working with traumatised children and attempting to implement therapeutic parenting.

1) **Lack of solution based training**- Carers say they are often given the theory about attachment, without any solutions about what they actually need to DO in particular situations.

For example local authorities and agencies, invest heavily in training which educates carers and staff about the causes of trauma, particularly around brain development, but carers report that they leave the training, return home to their children, and still have no clear strategy about how to deal with the presenting behaviours. They may also feel strongly that the trainer 'does not understand'.

2) **Lack of empathic support/ or proper understanding of Therapeutic Parenting/ attachment from professionals.** - At times this can be frustrating when professionals, unskilled in the area of developmental trauma and therapeutic parenting, deliberately or inadvertently undermine a boundary,

For example, if the boundary is that the child is not allowed to take her phone to the bedroom, a well-meaning professional, or member of extended family, might insist that it would be okay for a short time. This effectively makes the child feel unsafe and undermines the Therapeutic Parent.

"It is essential that the Therapeutic Parent is seen at all times, as an unassailable 'safe base' by the child".

Similarly, the strong enforcement of routines and boundaries can also be misinterpreted as rigidity and harshness by those outside of the family. Examples of this are in the video (b) 'What is Therapeutic Parenting'? *(Appendix B)*

In the example below, the carer is implementing therapeutic parenting. The strategies used are misunderstood, undermined and misinterpreted by other professionals. Where standard parenting techniques are championed, the Therapeutic Parent is likely to feel unsupported, angry, blamed and isolated. It is even more complex where numerous methodologies and parenting models are advised by various professionals, extended family and friends. Add to this the carer's own previous parenting experience and attachment style and it is easy to see how suddenly we have a vulnerable child conducting the orchestra of 'specialists'. Differing messages around parenting will also make the child feel unsafe, and may well lead to placement disruption, or even a catastrophic life event, as in the following example:

Case Study Paul & Mary

Experienced Foster Carer/ Therapeutic Parent Mary; Child Paul, aged 9.

Paul had reactive attachment disorder (disorganised attachment) with associated extreme behaviours and had been in placement with Mary for 7 years. Paul was responding well to Mary who was using therapeutic parenting techniques. Paul's behaviours included wetting, soiling, smearing, aggressive outbursts, cruelty to animals and other smaller children.

Mary, gave Paul one chocolate biscuit bar within his lunch box everyday as a treat. Paul stole all the biscuits and ate the packet. Using 'natural consequences' Mary told the child it was a shame he had chosen to eat all the biscuits in advance as now there were none left for the week. She replaced the biscuit with an extra piece of fruit.

Paul went to school and said he was hungry as Mary had not given him any lunch. (He had eaten it all on the way to school). Despite the fact that Mary had informed the school of her strategy regarding the chocolate biscuit, and likely reaction of Paul, the school informed the child's new social worker, Ann, that Paul was complaining that he had not been given lunch. Ann spoke to Paul. He told her he was never given any lunch and was always hungry. Ann was not aware that Paul's attachment difficulties meant that he found it difficult to tell when he was hungry, and when he was full. She did not speak to Mary about this and the school did not pass on information about the chocolate biscuit removal. Ann had not received sufficient training in attachment and trauma and was unaware that Paul often told 'sad stories', with himself as the victim, in order to ensure he was kept safe by the powerful adults he was talking to.

Ann visited Mary, with her manager to express 'extreme concerns' mainly centring on the packed lunches, and the fact that Mary would not break her own boundary of using 'natural consequences'. Mary explained what had happened, and also explained about the importance of natural consequences, but Ann insisted (in front of Paul), that Mary reinstated the chocolate biscuits. Mary's own supervising social worker (SSW) supported Mary and explained to Ann how this would undermine Mary and make Paul feel unsafe. Ann did not agree.

The situation worsened and after 3 months there was a strategy meeting, where there were found to be <u>no concerns</u> about Mary's care. By this time, Paul had begun escalating his behaviour dramatically, and manipulating Ann into overriding Mary's boundaries.

Ann ended the placement as she could not understand Mary's parenting techniques, citing Paul's deteriorating behaviour as the reason. With much stress and sadness, Paul was moved to a standard foster placement which lasted 2 days due to his extreme behaviours. He was then moved to a specialist residential therapeutic children's home.

At age 12, (3 years later), Paul was in a secure unit and told his new social worker that Mary had been the only person who had ever understood him and made him feel safe. At this point the new social worker attempted to contact Mary to see if Paul could be rehabilitated back to her. To her horror, she discovered that Mary had died of cancer a month earlier. She learnt that Mary had contacted Ann many times to try to maintain contact with Paul and eventually, to help him to say goodbye. Unfortunately Ann had maintained a punitive stance towards Mary and her therapeutic parenting style. She had refused to pass on any information to Paul. The impact on Paul was catastrophic, he believed he had been abandoned and he was unable to recover. He committed suicide 2 years later.

3) **Differing views of the child's personality/ behaviours** – As children who have suffered intense trauma are excellent at adapting their behaviours in order to survive, Therapeutic Parents are often frustrated and feel undermined when the 'fake smile' or adaptive behaviour is interpreted by others as the child's real persona. *This is explained more fully in video (a) 'Understanding your Traumatised Child' (link in Annex B).*

4) **Unrealistic expectations around timescales-** Many carers say that they were not aware how long it would take to begin to see real and significant

changes in the way their children think, and especially start to link cause and effect. This is especially challenging where supporting professionals and extended family also have unrealistic expectations. For example it is not unusual for carers to report education professionals stating that the child should be 'over' any earlier difficulties, after a 6 month period in a foster/ adoptive placement.

5) **Dealing with schools** – One of the major challenges a Therapeutic Parent faces, is getting the school on the same page. Schools, naturally, are very focused on results and education. Therapeutic parents are working first and foremost on relationship building, and starting to help the child build secure attachments. It is easy to see how sometimes homework would have to take a back seat, especially where the emotional age of the child is significantly younger, and there are difficulties in concentration. The case study above, Paul and Mary, also demonstrates how miscommunication and misunderstanding can quickly spiral into a circle of blame, resulting in unnecessary placement disruption. In our training, we always advise that school issues stay at school and vice versa. It is not possible for Therapeutic Parents to know exactly what transpired at school, and they risk de stabilising their relationship with the child if they inadvertently blame the child for something that was outside their control. A safer approach is to adopt a neutral stance, whilst not undermining the school- as in this, my own example;

Rosie was aged 16. She was sent home from school and I was informed that she had been 'very rude and aggressive' resulting in her exclusion for one day. In these situations it is tempting to 'tell the child off' and over punish. Thinking however, of triggers, I said, "I wonder what it was at school that made you so angry. Seems like you were scared"?

Using this open ended technique, Rosie was able to tell me that her teacher had been changed and she had not known who the person was. This was against her 'Statement of special educational needs'. I immediately understood the trigger for her fear based behaviour. Although I

> *supported the school in their exclusion as a 'natural consequence', my message to Rosie was, "I know you have a good heart and can sort this out. I have confidence in you". I then communicated the error that had been made to the school and explained the resulting behaviours to them.*

Some schools in the UK are now becoming more 'Attachment Aware' and we have been involved in re training many schools in adapting behavioural management techniques in the classroom. We always recommend Louise Bomber's book, 'Inside I'm Hurting' to schools, *(ref iv)* and to parents who are trying to engage their child' school in trauma and attachment related behaviours. It is interesting to note the high numbers of children being 'home schooled' who have attachment difficulties, alongside the instances of exclusion.

6) **Avoiding shame** – Therapeutic Parents are always aware how easily their child can be overwhelmed by shame or fear. The need to respond empathically as a default reaction, in order to avoid evoking shame and fear, can often feel at odds with the instinctive response. This is a daily struggle.

7) **Lack of practical resources**- Carers and parents have told us that they struggle to access the right resources for their children. Carers need to be able to access planners, 'fiddle' toys and appropriate children's story books to address the difficulties they are dealing with. These can often be found at sites providing equipment for children with ADHD, and Autism. We have found that many carers have found 'Chewelry' and 'now next later' prompt PEC cards particularly useful for children who have suffered early life trauma. We have a list of children's story books, which we have also found effective, in Appendix B

8) **Risk of false allegations**- As therapeutic parenting needs to be very 'boundaried' with strong routines, natural consequences and alternative strategies being used, we have seen (in Paul and Mary's case study), that it is possible that the parenting may be misinterpreted as 'harsh' when

safeguarding concerns may be raised. Sometimes allegations are unfounded and sometimes they are founded.

The 'sympathetic face'

With regards to false allegations, a particular difficulty is 'the sympathetic face'. Our children are hard wired to ensure their survival. When presented with a 'sympathetic face' our children often say whatever it takes to keep that face there, and keep themselves safe. IE

Child refuses to wear his coat to school. Child gets wet. Teaching Assistant meets chid with sympathetic face and says

"Oh dear! Poor you, you are soaked"!

Child, sees the sympathetic face, registers it subconsciously and needs to elicit more nurture so says,

"I haven't got a coat. Mum says I can't have one"

Cue allegation.

A simple shift in body language, facial expression and tone, along with good communication, can demonstrate nurture without leading to unfounded allegations.

In the next two chapters we will explore how we can create more joined up working, to overcome some of these additional challenges.

Chapter 5:
The impact of blocked care (compassion fatigue), and blame

One of the main challenges faced by social workers AND carers is the significant risk of the carer developing 'blocked care' or compassion fatigue. The strains and stresses of caring for children with attachment difficulties, the relentlessness of the behaviours and the lack of understanding regarding therapeutic parenting techniques, from those around the carer are significant risk factors.

When I went to research compassion fatigue in foster care, I was surprised to find that there was virtually no research worldwide. For this reason we undertook our own research with Bristol University in 2016. (Due for publication October 2016). At our training and conferences, we are well aware of the significant number of foster carers and adopters who come to the events and are suffering from compassion fatigue, or recognise that they have suffered from it in the past.

When parents and carers are caring for a child with difficult behaviours, arising from early life trauma, they lack positive reciprocal interactions. This places these carers at risk for gradually responding in a defensive manner. When a particular child consistently fails to respond to their caregiving, the carer is not 'rewarded' by caring for the child, therefore the carer is at risk of developing 'child specific' blocked care.

When compassion fatigue occurs, there are real physiological changes within the brain, which are beyond the carer's control. The carer is unable to access higher functioning, such as empathy, curiosity and applying new strategies. This makes it almost impossible for them to 'hear' and implement the very strategies which they need, at the time they need the most help.

The carer begins to feel ineffective and powerless. Their sense of failure is extremely stressful and they feel hopeless and helpless. In order to protect themselves they go into self-defence mode experiencing feelings of rejection and anger towards the child and others. When carers are experiencing blocked care, *'they are likely to experience little empathy for their children as they are not able to maintain a positive, reciprocal and satisfying relationship with the child. The carers approach, reward system is supressed and they eventually begin to focus on behaviour from a judgemental, critical stance'* (Hughes and Baylin 2012 ref iii)

Factors contributing to blocked care

The main contributing factor to blocked care is experiencing a high level of challenging behaviour, often based in early life trauma related behaviours. Carer report feeling 'ground down' with the relentless daily challenges. Sometimes these behavioural challenges appear frivolous and trivial to the outside world. It is the impact of these daily challenges, coupled with feeling unrewarded or even disliked as a parent which first drives the brain into 'self-defence' mode.

A carer who is beginning to experience blocked care, may be pushed further into this condition by unskilled professionals. This can happen a number of ways. Confusing empathy and sympathy, a lack of training or knowledge, and/ or minimising the problem in order to make it more 'manageable'. The diary entries later in this chapter, give examples of how this occurs. I often remind carers that social workers and their colleagues are motivated to help others but it is the lack of meaningful and relevant training which causes miscommunications.

Confusing empathy and sympathy

The next example demonstrates a common pitfall, fallen into with alarming regularity by those who do NOT live with children with attachment disorder/ early life developmental trauma. In order to try to demonstrate some empathy with the carer, or in a misguided attempt to help the 'solve the problem', the worker draws parallels between the carer's situation and their own. They might sympathise about how 'difficult teenagers can be', and add that they have a teenager of their own.

This is unlikely to be helpful to the carer. In fact it can have the opposite effect, making it clear to the parent that the helping professional has no real idea about what they are dealing with, increasing their feelings of isolation, and contributing to the risk of a placement disruption. The Therapeutic Parent is raising <u>different</u> children, and in order to strengthen the relationship between parent and helper, supporting professionals <u>must acknowledge and accept that difference</u>.

> "A professional telling a therapeutic parent that they 'know how they feel', as they also have a teenager, is the same as saying we know what it is to be blind as we sometimes close our eyes: There really is NO comparison".

Lack of training or knowledge, and /or minimising the 'problem'

In the following three extracts from emails, the professional has not received sufficient training, so the problem is either not recognised or minimised, leaving the carer feeling isolated and misunderstood.

Example 1: Adopter of three siblings, all with attachment difficulties/ developmental trauma of varying extremes, in placement 10 years (Leon 13, and Polly 11, had had a very antagonistic, well documented, often violent relationship for almost 9 years).

> *Discussion today with social worker about sibling rivalry. We had had to build Leon a bedroom on a different level of the house so that he and Polly were never unsupervised due to the levels of aggression and violence. The social worker knew this and still said...*
>
> *"The thing is all brothers and sisters fight sometimes don't they? I mean it is quite normal. I remember once my brother threw my favourite doll down the stairs just out of spite"!*
>
> *I replied, (with a blank face and quiet voice), "No, it is not the same. Do you know about attachment difficulties at all and how that impacts on sibling relationships?"'*
>
> *This social worker said she did not hold with 'all that American stuff'. I thought about giving up. I can't continue in this vacuum of ignorance. I know that she basically thinks I am imagining it all or making it up. Sometimes I think she wants the problems to be tiny and 'normal' so she can solve them. I wish she would just admit she doesn't have a clue either!!*

Example 2: Adopter of 4 siblings with extreme attachment difficulties, learning difficulties, foetal alcohol spectrum disorder, 10 years into placement. (Children suffered extreme deprivation cruelty and neglect in early life. The adopter sought independent advice from a child psychiatrist).

> *I can't believe that I got the report through today (from the child psychiatrist) and it says...*
>
> *'As Saffron was removed (from extreme neglect and abuse) at the age of 18 months she will have no conscious memory of her early life and is unlikely to have any difficulties in the future'.*
>
> *What chance do I have of trying to make his teacher understand why I am doing therapeutic parenting with this kind of statement? I have emailed the psychiatrist but he says he 'doesn't discuss reports'.*

Example 3: From foster carer complaint. Child in placement Kieran with attachment disorder, age 15, in placement 12 years.

> *Social Worker (visiting at time of intense trauma in the family): So how old was Kieran when he came to live with you?*
>
> *Me: Three and a half.*
>
> *Social Worker: And he is now 15?*
>
> *Me: Yes that's right.*
>
> *Social Worker: So he won't really remember anything, so his behaviour now is nothing to do with any early trauma. (Subtext; it is all your fault)*
>
> *Me; (experiencing a 'falling sensation'): Do you know about attachment difficulties and related behaviour?*
>
> *(She didn't).*
>
> *After this exchange I felt like everything that Kieran did was basically down to me. I felt I could do no more for him. Luckily I had a good supportive adoption team social worker who knew about attachment. She was able to reassure me and the adoption didn't disrupt. If she had not been there I would have thrown in the towel.*

The Circle of Blame

When a placement is in jeopardy, the supporting social workers, therapists, teachers etc. will naturally be focussed on preserving the placement if that is appropriate, however at the very time when the carer needs to hear and accept strategies, blocked care will make this difficult or impossible to do. This leads to what we describe as the 'circle of blame'.

"It is misunderstandings, unrealistic expectations and lack of knowledge which combine to form the foundation stone of blocked care -BLAME"

Looking after children who have suffered early life trauma is extremely difficult for EVERYONE. Carers look to supporting professionals for answers around the challenging behaviours, but often the answers are not easy to find and some professionals may fall back onto old tried and trusted parenting methods which are working with their own children but largely ineffective with traumatised children. The professional may begin to feel de skilled when their strategies do not work. It is at these times that the professional sometimes falls into the trap of blaming the carer, for 'not listening' or ineffective implementation of strategies. The carer may also be blamed for a perceived lack of empathy or warmth, due to blocked care.

At the same time, the carer feels alone and judged. He or she may see the child as the root cause of all their troubles. If they are not skilled in therapeutic parenting, or they are deep into compassion fatigue, they may well withdraw from the child or express negative fear based statements such as;

"Nothing we do makes any difference"!

'I think he is schizophrenic'!

"She is pure evil"

These statements rightly elicit a protective response from supporters and professionals... protective towards the child and perhaps exasperation towards the carer. We must remember that the visiting professional sees only the very tip of the 'challenging behaviour iceberg', whilst the carer has a 'wet suit' on for most of the time.

(Fig 3) The Circle of Blame

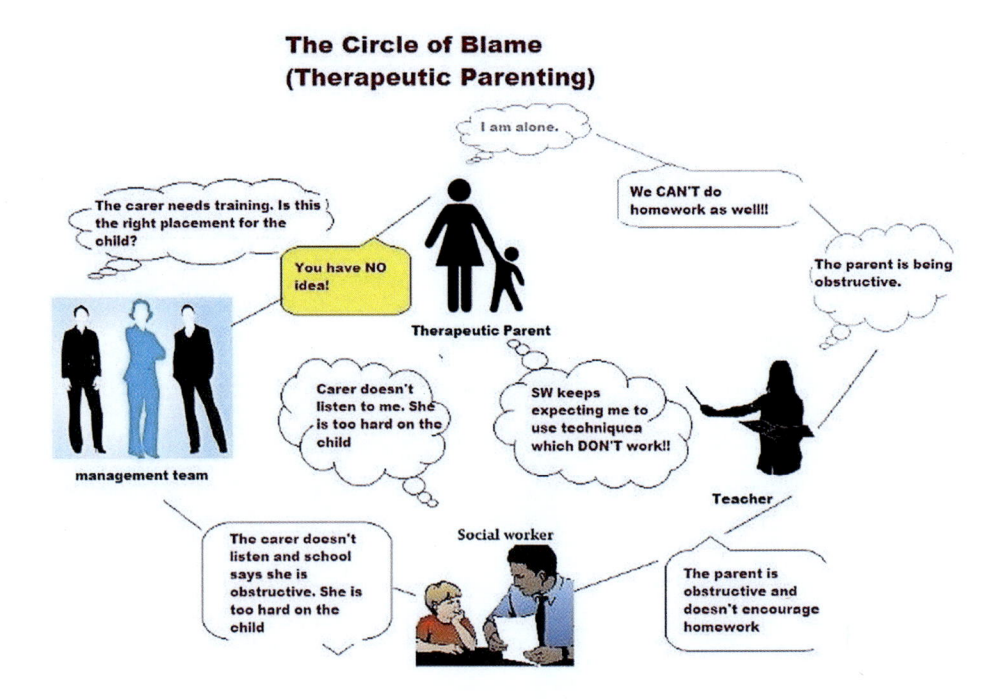

The Circle of Blame (Therapeutic Parenting)

- I am alone.
- We CAN'T do homework as well!!
- The carer needs training. Is this the right placement for the child?
- You have NO idea!
- The parent is being obstructive.
- Therapeutic Parent
- management team
- Carer doesn't listen to me. She is too hard on the child
- SW keeps expecting me to use techniques which DON'T work!!
- Teacher
- Social worker
- The carer doesn't listen and school says she is obstructive. She is too hard on the child
- The parent is obstructive and doesn't encourage homework

It is common for the carer to see the social worker or therapist as the source of the problem and then also to blame them for 'not listening' or 'not understanding'. Sometimes this blame is founded, and whilst understandable, is never useful.

> "At the centre of the 'circle of blame' is a traumatised child whose every move is misinterpreted or over analysed".

The 'misunderstanding gap', which we often refer to in our training, happens when the well-meaning supporting professional, is inadequately trained or supported themselves in the effects of early life trauma. I know, I was one!

Naturally, the social worker's job is to keep the interests of the child at the heart of their work. When carers are beginning to enter blocked care, a knee jerk 'fix all' solution is sometimes thought to be a placement move for the child. Not only, however, is this likely to be extremely damaging for the child AND the carer, but in the long run, it is usually the precursor to multiple moves, where behaviours are not understood, and further damage is done to the child's frail attachments.

What do we DO about blocked care?

A simple shift by a social worker, therapist, or any other supporter can maintain the placement, build the relationship and avoid all the work and heartache that an unplanned move entails. Use of the T.R.U.E. model within the agency or local authority will assist in protecting the child, supporting the carer to stay out of blocked care, AND also support the social worker in their tasks. This is explained in Chapter 6.

Compassion and empathy (*not sympathy*) helps to shift the carer's brain from defence mode, which allows them to access higher brain functions, re igniting their capacity for empathy, self-regulation and a return to therapeutic parenting. Empathy for the carer effectively lowers the stress hormones which are blocking the brain, and preventing the carer accessing their own empathy for the child.

It may be necessary for the carer to have respite for a few days, in order to be able to shift from defence towards empathic responding. In our own agency, we found the most effective respite was encouraging the Therapeutic Parent to leave the home, while the respite carers, (usually highly trained close friends or family) moved in. This lessened interruptions to routine and boundaries, avoided the child feeling rejected and considerably reduced anxiety based behaviours leading up to and from the respite period.

It is important that work is done with the Therapeutic Parent DURING the respite period to re awaken the caring part of the brain, with sensitive, brain based intervention. In order to begin the process of 'unblocking' the carer's brain they need to feel safe, understood and not criticised for the feelings they have. In turn this reawakens feelings of care and empathy for the child, and the placement may be maintained or restored. The carer can be helped to 'remember' strategies which were effective in the past. Sometimes the most useful thing a supporting professional or friend can say is,

"I can't imagine how difficult this must be at the moment."

Although the social worker may well consider that the carer is experiencing blocked care, and take action around this, clearly the overriding factor must be the safety of the child. It may be difficult for inexperienced professionals to judge, what is simply strong but effective, therapeutic parenting and what is emotionally abusive.

The practitioner who is advocating for the child and ensuring their best interests are at the forefront of practice, must be;

- Skilled in interpreting the child's verbal and non-verbal messages. This is especially relevant where the child has attachment difficulties.

- Aware of their own body language (beware the 'sympathetic face')

- Knowledgeable about the therapeutic parenting techniques being used

- Able to present the child's view alongside that of the Supervising Social Worker, supporting the therapeutic placement.

Course (h) *for carers and supporting professionals, (link in Appendix B)* –'Re-establishing inner peace, reconnecting to your child', and Course (j) for supporting professionals, mentors etc. 'Recognising, Understanding and Managing Compassion Fatigue', are available online for carers and professionals.

The T.R.U.E model (in the following chapter) is based on this empathic cornerstone of therapeutic parenting and helps to avoid, recognise and resolve blocked care.

Chapter 6

The T.R.U.E model of support and intervention

Implementing meaningful support for Therapeutic Parents and avoiding/ alleviating blocked care

T.R.U.E stands for;

- Therapeutic

- Re-parenting

- Underpinned by

- Experience / Empathy

In 2010 I developed and implemented the 'T.R.U.E' model of therapeutic parenting, within my former fostering agency. These methods compliment the P.A.C.E (Dan Hughes) model and ensures <u>affective</u> empathy is extended and available to the therapeutic parent.

In November 2013 Ofsted inspected our agency and fully evaluated the T.R.U.E therapeutic model in place. The agency was awarded 'Outstanding' as a result. Ofsted stated;

> *The overriding emphasis of the care provided focuses on promoting children's well-being, this helps them to make exceptional progress. The service….has developed a **therapeutic model of support where up to three workers from the agency support the carer and the children in placement. This has been closely evaluated and received very positively by social workers and child care professionals.** It is excellent practice which is welcomed and highly valued by foster carers.*
>
> *Local authority commissioners comment very favourably regarding the positive outcomes for children who are placed with carers of the service. For example one manager stated, 'our **children have made exceptional and highly unexpected progress** and if all services operated like this one there would be a lot less unplanned endings.'*

The T.R.U.E model requires the Therapeutic Parent to have EASY access to a supporter who truly understands and empathises with their task. This may be another foster carer, adopter or someone who has been specifically trained. This 'affective empathy' is very powerful in helping to resolve blocked care. The carer feels heard and understood. The sense of blame and isolation diminishes. Chemical changes happen in the brain which enable the carer to re access 'higher thinking' such as empathy and strategies they have used successfully in the past.

In the T.R.U.E. model there are **three main supporters** around the family.

1) **Attachment Worker (AW)** – The T.R.U.E model requires a specialist in attachment, with DIRECT personal experience of living with children with attachment difficulties. An empathic supporter must be available to the carer of the child, by someone who has had direct experience of therapeutic parenting themselves. Specialist mentoring, ie from another trained foster carer or adopter, goes some way to assisting in this. The AW MUST be trained in recognising and managing blocked care, and also in attachment related behaviours. Ideally the AW may also be DDP trained. (Dyadic Developmental Psychotherapy, Dan Hughes). The AW works alongside the Supervising Social Worker, and only works directly with the

parent, not the child. Their main role is to establish an early empathic relationship with the carer, preferably before the child even comes in to placement. This type of support builds resilience in the carer and helps to sustain difficult placements. The AW is supervised by a senior attachment worker, possibly a therapist or therapeutic social worker, and **not** by the Supervising Social worker. This helps to avoid blame and promotes objectivity, and solution based problem solving, where there is blocked care. The AW does NOT need social work qualifications.

2) **Child Support Worker (CSW)** – The CSW has a longstanding relationship with the child and sees them regularly, normally weekly or fortnightly. Often the CSW will be qualified in child care or have a background in advocating for children in the care system. The CSW will ideally be trained in life story work, Theraplay and have attended training in therapeutic parenting techniques, early life trauma, attachment difficulties, P.A.C.E and blocked care, (compassion fatigue). The CSW is a good advocate for the child and is able to maintain a longstanding relationship with them, even where there are placement changes, either permanently, or through respite arrangements. The CSW liaises closely with the child's own social worker as well as the AW and SSW. 20 years ago, the CSW tasks were regularly undertaken by the child's social worker, however with changes in statutory duties, increased workloads and report writing, this role is often better served by a professional who ONLY has advocating, as a main role.

3) **Supervising Social Worker (SSW).** The SSW is responsible for all statutory targets and obligations being met. They must also be knowledgeable about therapeutic parenting techniques, developmental trauma and attachment difficulties, and be able to support the carer in the implementation of strategies. The SSW will liaise closely with the AW who is able to work more intensively with the carer to help prevent blocked care. The SSW is responsible for supervising the CSW, but not the AW. As the SSW has the AW working alongside, they have more time to discuss and

implement training needs, regulatory issues, safe caring and other essential elements in preserving the placement.

This model relies on EXCELLENT communication by all parties, indicated by the blue arrows. Electronic recording, uploaded to a central accessible server, facilitates this. (fig 3)

Fig 4 The T.R.U.E. Model of support and intervention

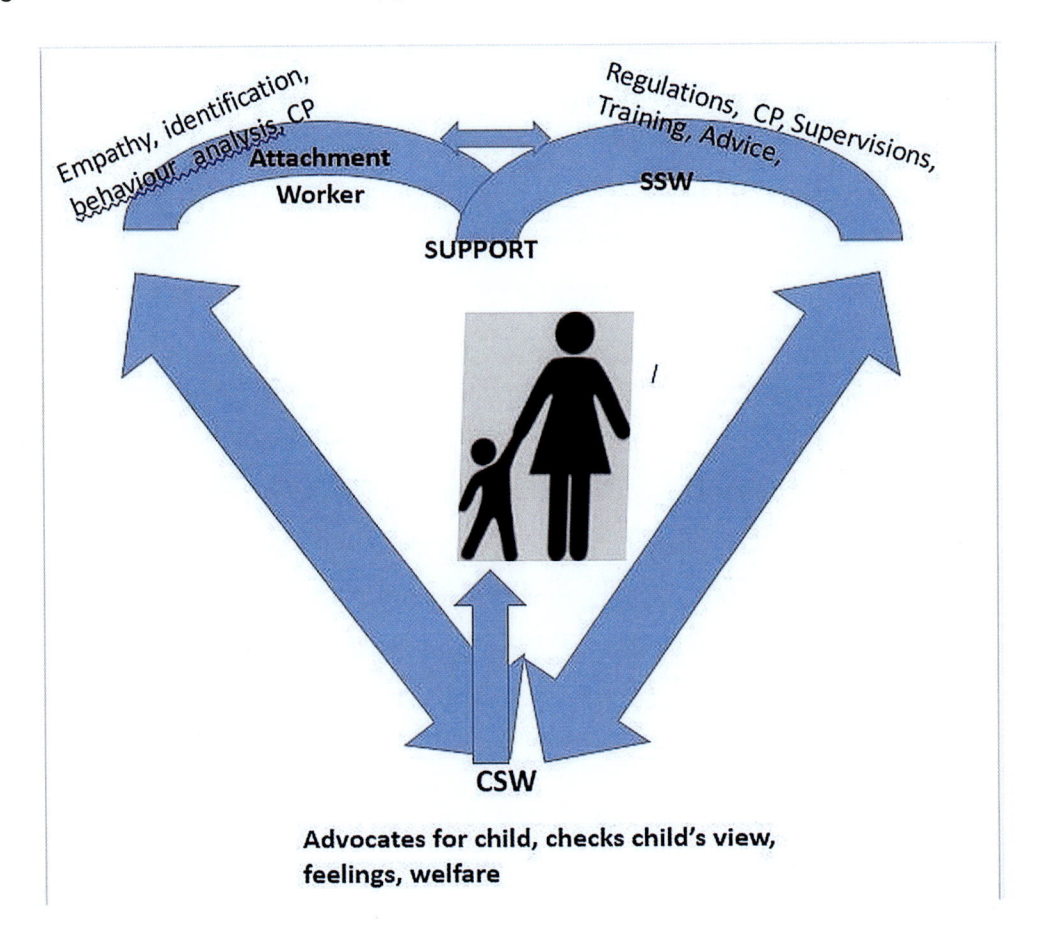

Empathy, identification, behaviour analysis, CP
Attachment Worker

Regulations, CP Supervisions, Training, Advice,
SSW

SUPPORT

CSW
Advocates for child, checks child's view, feelings, welfare

The T.R.U.E model helps to engage supporting professionals and carers more closely, and implements joined up therapeutic parenting support for the child. Other training or intervention is also effective and can be used alongside the T.R.U.E model. These include the Dyadic Developmental Psychotherapy model, or formal training/ workshops around compassion fatigue for carers.

Conclusion

Therapeutic Parenting is a different way of life for foster carers, adopters and other parents who are caring for children who have suffered trauma. The children they are caring for have often been neglected and abused and are very likely to exhibit signs of attachment difficulty. This may affect <u>every aspect</u> of the child's life <u>long term</u> and have a profound impact on the carer.

The Therapeutic Parent uses enhanced parenting, underpinned by empathy, nurture, clear routines, boundaries and natural consequences. This enables the child to begin to link cause and effect and form new pathways in their brain, assisting them, (over a prolonged period of time), to make attachments and begin to trust adults. Dan Hugh's P.A.C.E model is a recognised therapeutic model, currently used and promoted in the UK.

Some standard parenting techniques are not used in Therapeutic Parenting, as they may replicate early abuse. They may also rely on the child's ability to self-regulate. This is unrealistic.

One of the biggest challenges faced by Therapeutic Parents, is the lack of understanding from supporting professionals in their task. The parent may be undermined in their parenting by well-meaning others. This often leads to the carer experiencing, isolation, blame, anger and frustration and can also contribute to blocked care, (compassion fatigue). Where the traumatised child experiences conflict between the parent and supporting professionals, this will inevitably lead to her feeling unsafe, and ultimately to placement disruption.

Social Workers need to be able to access and implement relevant guidance and training in;

- recognising and working with children with attachment difficulties, therapeutic parenting strategies, and

- identifying and managing blocked care, in order to assist therapeutic parents in avoiding placement disruption an achieving better outcomes for children.

The T.R.U.E model of care is an effective model to support both Therapeutic Parents AND Social Workers in their task, and has achieved excellent outcomes regarding placement stability for children.

Therapeutic parenting is most effective if the whole team around the child are on board. This requires co-operation, insight, empathy and understanding from schools, therapists, social workers, fostering or adoption agencies extended family, and anyone else working alongside the family.

The Therapeutic Parent **must be enabled** to be the unassailable 'safe base' in the child's eyes, in order to ensure the **best chance** for the child to heal.

Therapeutic Parenting - the difference between 'no hope' and 'every chance'.

Appendix A-
Therapeutic Parenting differences- quick reference chart

Difference #	Explanation	Why the Child Needs This 'Difference'
#1 Therapeutic Parenting is different to standard parenting	Standard 'good parenting' does not go far enough in HEALING the child. Some standard parenting responses are unhelpful to traumatised children. Significant change may not be achievable for MANY years. The Therapeutic Parent (TP) carefully manages the base brain of the child in order to assist the child in self-regulating and avoiding shame. Standard, 'good parenting' assumes a basic level of security, empathy, resilience and self-regulation, which is simply not present in the traumatised child.	The children have often been neglected and/or abused and are very likely to exhibit signs of attachment difficulty. Typically the child may over react, be aggressive, over controlling, hypersensitive, have difficulty in sensing hunger, pain, have overwhelming shame and fear of abandonment. This may be all consuming. Children with attachment difficulties (AD) have heightened 'fight/flight' responses, due to their base brain being 'in charge'. If we think of their base brain as over active smoke detectors, their 'smoke detectors' are always going off, even when there is no danger. The child needs a different kind of parenting to help them to build new pathways, (synapses) in the brain, and 'regulate the 'smoke detector'.

#2 Therapeutic parenting has strong routines and boundaries	The TP will implement a strong routine from the outset. This strong routine is largely inflexible. The TP is unlikely to act spontaneously as routine and predictability are key to the child's feelings of security, i.e. meal times are normally very fixed with everybody sitting at the same place at the table. Children would also have their own cutlery and crockery assigned to them. Boundaries will also be very firm. The TP cannot allow a child to do something today, which he was not allowed to do yesterday, or vice versa. Any changes to boundaries need to be done slowly and carefully as the child develops. Surprises and spontaneity are avoided.	This allows the child to feel safe and to be able to predict their life events, maybe for the first time. Having an identified 'place' means this child is able to identify their space in the world, and the fear of 'invisibility' lessens. Having a strong boundaries lessens the children's stress response, keeps their fight flight 'smoke detector' response under control, and ensures a safe predictable environment. A 'surprise' would normally lead to higher levels of cortisol, resulting in fear and dysregulation.
#3 The use of natural or life consequences.	The TP will allow the child to experience 'natural or life consequences' For example the child may choose to spend all the pocket money instantly. The carer would not intervene and lend additional money if a sudden urgent 'need' for more money was discovered!	This enables the child to begin to link cause and effect and forms new pathways in their brain, assisting them, (over a prolonged period of time), to understand the consequences of their actions and start to moderate their behaviour. **Unrelated consequences** – i.e. writing lines, do not help the child to link cause and effect, and are likely to increase conflict

		between the carer and child.
4 The rejection of exclusion	Planned ignoring, time out, naughty step, sending to room and other excluding/ withdrawal methods, are not used in therapeutic parenting.

Instead a TP may use time in, where the child is asked to 'stay close' to the carer, so they can be 'kept safe' at times of dysregulation. | The child may strongly fear abandonment and 'being invisible' or forgotten.

Exclusion may replicate early abusive situations, and places a reliance on the child being able to self-regulate. This is unrealistic. The child needs assistance from the TP to self- regulate and re attune. |
| **#5 Expecting too much from the child.** | The TP avoids asking the child why they behaved in a certain way. Generally the TP would not be spending long periods of time talking to the child in depth about their behaviour,

Saying sorry- the TP would not expect or insist on any kind of meaningful apology from a traumatised child. Instead **Making it right/ showing sorry is used.** The TP gives the child opportunities to 'make things right' and 'show sorry'. For example if objects were thrown, the child would be expected and 'helped' to pick them up. | The child is unable to provide the answers and may feel more fearful and experience heightened shame if they are asked to provide explanations to the TP.

As the child is likely to say 'what the carer wants to hear', without facilitating any fundamental change to the behaviour, saying sorry is an unsatisfactory resolution for both carer and child. |
| **#6 The use of empathy and acceptance** | The TP uses empathy to first establish a connection to the child and to reflect back to them what they are experiencing i.e. 'I can see you are finding this difficult'.

Conscious/ empathic response – The TP practices responding to children in a measured and | In order to connect to the child and 'shift' them from dysregulation and overwhelming shame, the empathic connection gets quickly to the heart of the matter without provoking a fight flight |

	thoughtful manner, without acting on sometimes overwhelming feelings of anger i.e. Child says 'I hate you' empathic response would be; 'It must be really difficult to feel that you hate me'. **Acceptance** –The therapeutic parent has to go much further to accept the child, but not the behaviours. The behaviours are more entrenched, more frequent and often very difficult to understand. Using phrases such as 'I know you have a good heart, so I was really surprised that you…..' are effective.	response.
#7 Rewards and Praise	Therapeutic parents would avoid punishing a child by removing an important reward or treat. The TP would still give consequences for any negative behaviours but would make the child aware that they thought them 'worthy' of such a reward, even though the child was 'doing their best' to have it taken away. The TP avoids 'over praising' the traumatised child. For example, if the child produced a drawing, the carer would not say it was 'wonderful' and place it in a position of pride. This may well lead to the child destroying the picture. The TP gives a muted interested response, such as, *'That's an interesting picture, what is that bit there'?* Generally the TP would avoid reward and star charts. This can cause conflict where they are widely used in a child's school.	The child's internal working model (IWM) may be comfortable with being 'unworthy' of the treat. The child may therefore attempt to sabotage it, thereby reminding the carer of their 'badness'. Over praising can cause conflict with the child's internal working model. This may lead the child to feeling that the carer is lying or unsafe. If the child's IWM is comfortable 'in the wrong', star charts are an unhelpful daily reminder of irresolvable conflict.

#8 Recognising and changing survival strategies	The TP recognises and gently challenges survival strategies such as fake smile, assimilation, nonsense chatter, baby voice. For example- The TP will make a distinction between 'nonsense chatter/ questions and genuine expressed thoughts and feelings. The carer will also help the child to regulate themselves and reduce 'nonsense chatter', by perhaps asking them to write the questions down, or devoting a small part of the day to listening to the 'nonsense chatter'	Children with attachment difficulties are often very adept at assimilating by reading facial signals of others and quickly adapting their behaviour to ensure their own survival. An inexperienced carer or professional may misinterpret this as manipulation. The behaviours are deep seated and may continue long after any threat has passed. By helping the child to become aware of their own behaviours, and the impact on others, the child learns a degree of self-control.
#9 Use of Curiosity and Naming the need	The TP will always be aware of the child's early life experiences and help them to make sense of the resulting behaviours by 'naming the need' *This is explained in the video –* Naming the Need http://youtu.be/JMBtepk_MZE TPs can use a third party story where they feel the child would be too overwhelmed by linking current behaviours to earlier specific events.	Naming the need, gives the child insight and control. They are able to understand and link their own behaviours. This usually leads to a significant change in negative behaviours, often quite quickly.
#10 Use of Playfulness	Most parents will be playful with their children at appropriate times. The TP, purposefully uses a playful response where they notice a child is dysregulated. Playfulness in this way is NOT about 'playing' with the child. It is a spontaneous, unexpected 'silly' intervention.	The child can not feel fear and joy simultaneously, so by instigating a joyful response the fear, underpinning the dysregulation is diminished.

Appendix B –Author's own resources: <u>Video and web links</u>

Inspire Training Group www.inspiretraininggroup.com
(Part of Fostering Attachments Ltd)

Video a: Understanding Your Traumatised Child
https://m.youtube.com/watch?v=o-IYlkDlkgk

Video b: What is Therapeutic Parenting?
https://m.youtube.com/watch?feature=youtu.be&v=Y-oWUZNhEXo

Video c: Contrasting emotional response with conscious/ empathic response
http://youtu.be/PksUFUMFUfY

Video d: An Empathic Response
https://m.youtube.com/watch?feature=youtu.be&v=6omZr5BKEz0&rdm=1s4usxx6&client=mv-google

Video e: Naming the Need
http://youtu.be/JMBtepk_MZE

Video Course f: 'Therapeutic Parenting P.A.C.E in Real Life' Full online training course with certificate. https://fosteringattachments.learnupon.com/store/91417-therapeutic-parenting-pace-in-real-life?tab=1

Video g Tutorial: How to Deal with Nonsense Chatter
https://fosteringattachments.learnupon.com/store/59264-3-how-to-deal-with-nonsense-chatter?tab=1

Online Video Course h: Intervention to help carers overcome compassion fatigue/ blocked care. https://fosteringattachments.learnupon.com/store/58682-re-estabilising-inner-peace-re-connecting-with-your-child?tab=1

Video Course j: 'Recognising, Managing and Resolving Compassion Fatigue (blocked care) for Supporting Professionals', with certificate.
https://fosteringattachments.learnupon.com/store/91104-recognising-understanding-and-managing-compassion-fatigue-for-professionals?tab=1

Appendix C: References and bibliography

I. Building the Bonds of Attachment, Awakening Love in Deeply Troubled children, Dan Hughes. Publisher -Jason Aronson
II. Nurturing Attachments *Supporting Children who are Fostered or Adopted* **(2008) p.205 Natural Consequences** Kim Golding. Jessica Kingsley Publishers
III. Brain Based Parenting: the neuroscience of caregiving for healthy attachment, Jonathan Baylin and Dan Hughes 2012 p.133. Norton series.
IV. Inside I'm Hurting, (for schools). Louise Bomber. Worth Publishing
V. Attachment Handbook for Foster Carers and Adopters- Schofield and Beek (2009)
VI. The Body Keeps the Score- Dr Bessel Van der Kolk. Penguin 2015
VII. Why Can't My Child Behave? Empathic parenting strategies for foster carers and adopters. Dr Amber Elliot. Jessica Kingsley Publishers.
VIII. The Whole Brain Child. Dr Daniel Seigal. Robinson 2012

IX. Woolgar M (2013) 'The Practical Implications of the Emerging Findings in the Neurobiology of Maltreatment for Looked After and Adopted Children:
X. Dr Bruce Perry http://attachmentdisorderhealing.com/developmental-trauma-2/ Bruce Perry effects of trauma on brain.
XI. Adoption UK training evaluation 2009 Hadley Centre for Adoption and Foster Care Studies with University of Bristol and the Evaluation Trust;
XII. Early brain development and maltreatment. Department for Education 2014 UK. http://fosteringandadoption.rip.org.uk/topics/early-brain-development/
XIII. Compassion Fatigue in Foster Care: Inspire Training, Fostering Attachments Ltd with Hadley Centre for Adoption and Foster Care Studies with University of Bristol. UK study October 2016.
XIV. Early childhood Trauma Dept. for Education Research in Practice http://fosteringandadoption.rip.org.uk/topics/early-childhood-trauma/

Recommended Therapeutic Parenting Children's Books
XV. The Boy who built a wall around himself. Ali Redford. Jessica Kingsley Publishers
XVI. William Wobbly and the Very Bad Day: Sophie Spikey has a Very Big Problem
Rosie Rudey and the Very Annoying Parent: Charley Chatty and the Wiggly Worry Worm: All four books by Sarah Naish & Rosie Jefferies- Jessica Kingsley Publishers. October 2016
XVII. The Day the Sea Went Out, and never came back. Margot Sunderland.
XVIII. Speechmark Publishing Ltd. How are you feeling today Baby Bear? Jane Evans, Jessica Kingsley Publishers